SCHOLASTIC

Hands-On History

IMMIGRATION

by Michael Gravois

New York • Toronto • London • Auckland • Sydney
Mexico City • New Delhi • Hong Kong • Buenos Aires

Teaching Resources

Dedication

To my grandparents—
Gaston and May Gravois
and Paul and Amelia Lucker—
and to their parents before them

Cover design by Jason Robinson
Interior design by Michael Gravois
Interior illustrations by Jim Palmer
Photo Acknowledgements
The photographs are reproduced with the permission of:
Corbis, p. 12; National Park Service care of Holiday House, p. 14;
Library of Congress, p. 17 (top and middle), p. 39 (top left and middle left); Bettmann/Corbis, p. 17 (bottom), p. 39 (bottom left);
William Williams Paper/New York Public Library, p. 39 (top right); Alexander Alland Collection/Culver, p. 39 (bottom right)

ISBN 0-439-41124-6

Copyright © 2004 by Michael Gravois. All rights reserved.

Printed in the U.S.A.

1 2 3 4 5 6 7 8 9 10   40   11 10 09 08 07 06 05 04

Table of Contents

Introduction

As a middle-school teacher, I was always looking for ways to keep students interested and enthusiastic about learning. I developed activities and projects that helped me teach the required curriculum and also made my lessons fun, hands-on, diverse, and challenging.

I used an interactive-project approach with my fifth-grade students, and I can't stress enough how much they enjoyed it. Throughout each unit I had my students keep the activity sheets and projects in a pocket folder, so they could assemble a student-made textbook on the subject we were studying. They used these textbooks as a study guide for the final test. I was amazed at the higher-level thinking that took place in class discussions and by the degree of knowledge the students had acquired by the end of each unit. Parents even commented on the unique way the information was presented and how easy it was for their children to study for the final test. After seeing my students' success, I decided to put my ideas on paper. *Hands-On History: Immigration* is a compilation of the activities I used to teach immigration.

For each activity and project, I've included detailed instructions. Many of the activities incorporate language arts and critical thinking skills, such as public speaking, point of view, comparing and contrasting, understanding cause and effect, writing a letter, brainstorming, and sequencing.

I hope your students enjoy these projects as much as mine did.

How to Use This Book

Supplies

At the beginning of the school year, ask students to bring in the materials needed to create projects throughout the year. Also arrange the classroom desks into clusters, each with a bin to hold pens, pencils, markers, glue sticks, scissors, and other needed supplies. This enables students to share the materials. Have each of your students bring in the following materials:

- a roll of scotch tape
- several glue sticks
- a good pair of scissors
- a packet of colored pencils
- a packet of thin, colored markers
- a project folder (pocket-type) to hold papers and other project materials

Maximizing Learning

Because students have different learning styles, you may want to first orally summarize the information you will be covering on a given day. Then you can read the related section in the textbook or trade book. Finally, have students complete the activity. This not only exposes visual, aural, and artistic learners to the information through their strongest learning style, but it also allows all students to review the same information several times.

Home/School Communication

Before beginning a new unit with my class, I send a letter home to parents informing them of the upcoming unit and requesting their help, in case any of them have a special skill related to the subject we are studying. Here is a sample of the letter I send to the parents.

Dear _____

    For the next few weeks, our social studies curriculum will focus on the immigration movement in America, specifically from 1860 to 1910. We will study the reasons for immigration, cultural influences of these new citizens, recipes brought over from other countries, famous immigrants, important landmarks such as Ellis Island and the Statue of Liberty, and the nature of prejudice. While we study this era, your child will be introduced to quality literature that reflects life during this incredible growth spurt in America's history.

    If anyone in your family is a first-generation immigrant, please ask if he or she would like to visit our class to share his or her story. If you know tales of your ancestors' journeys, please share them with your child so that he or she can tell them to the class. Or better yet, feel free to visit our class and relate your stories directly.

    As usual, I ask that if you have any novels, photography books, memorabilia, or other items related to the immigration theme, please consider allowing your child to bring them to class. Make sure that your name is on any items brought to class.

    Thank you for your help. If you have any questions or suggestions, or would like to make an appointment to visit our class, you can reach me at [telephone number].

Sincerely,

Immigration Vocabulary Bulletin Board

Materials: brown and blue construction paper, copies of pages 32 and 33, colored markers, scissors, stapler

At the beginning of your immigration unit, set up a vocabulary bulletin board that students can add to as the unit unfolds. Use strips of brown paper for the ground and blue paper for the sky, and add a title banner that reads "Foreign Vocabulary." Keep a supply of vocabulary immigrant templates handy for students to use. Have students take turns writing each new vocabulary word and its definition on the suitcase of a different immigrant as they learn it. Then ask students to color the figure, cut it out, and add it to the bulletin board. See the list on page 6 for possible words to use and their definitions.

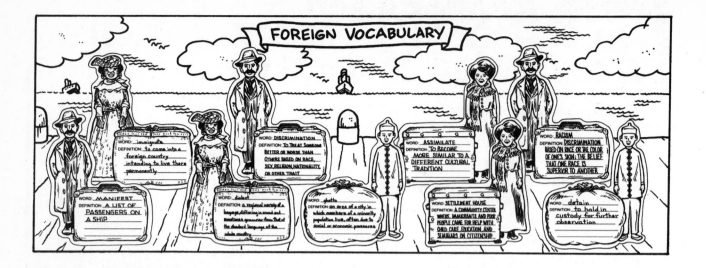

Suggested Vocabulary Words

assimilate: to become more similar to a different cultural tradition

detain: to hold in custody for further observation

dialect: a regional variety of a language, differing in sound and sometimes grammar from that of the standard language of the whole country

discrimination: treating someone better or worse than others based on race, sex, religion, nationality, or other trait

emigrate: to leave one's country to settle elsewhere

ghetto: an area of a city in which members of a minority population live, often due to social or economic pressures

illiterate: unable to read or write

immigrate: to come into a foreign country intending to live there permanently

manifest: a list of passengers on a ship

prejudice: a feeling, without basis, that one group is better or worse than another group

quarantine: the act of keeping a sick person away from healthy people to prevent the spread of disease

racism: discrimination based on race or the color of one's skin; the belief that one race is superior to another

settlement house: a community center where immigrants and poor people came for help with child care, education, and seminars on citizenship

tenement: a building that is divided into small apartments

Seven Reasons for Immigration Mini-Book

Materials: copier paper, scissors, colored markers or pencils

There are many reasons why a person or family would choose to leave their homeland and settle in America. Ask students to brainstorm reasons why people might have immigrated to America in the past, and list their responses on the board.

Then give students paper and show them how to fold it into a mini-book, following the directions below. Ask students to write a title for their mini-book on the cover (one that includes their name), such as, "Mela's Mini-Book of Immigration." On each of the following seven pages—including the back cover—have students write one of the reasons at the top of the page, draw an icon representing the reason, and then add a complete sentence describing that reason.

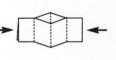

CREATING THE MINI-BOOK

1. Instruct students to fold a sheet of paper in half, as shown.

2. Have them fold it in half again in the same direction.

3. Then tell students to fold this long, narrow strip in half in the opposite direction.

4. Ask them to open up the paper to the Step 2 position and cut halfway down the vertical fold.

5. Students can open the paper and turn it horizontally. There should be a hole in the center where the cut was made.

6. Ask them to fold the paper in half lengthwise.

7. Then show students how to push in on the ends of the paper so the slit opens up. They should push until the center panels meet.

8. Finally, have students fold the four pages into a mini-book, flipping through the pages so that the cover is on the outside, and then crease the binding.

Suggested Answers for Mini-Books

TO FIND WORK:
Many people, such as Italians and Asians, wanted to escape economic difficulties, poverty, and unemployment. They thought of America as the "Land of Opportunity."

IN SEARCH OF RELIGIOUS FREEDOM:
Some people, such as Jews and Protestants, came to escape religious persecution. Today America is made up of people of many faiths.

TO ESCAPE AN OPPRESSIVE GOVERNMENT:
Some governments, such as the Russian government in the 19th century, seriously limited the freedom of its people. America is known as the "Land of the Free."

TO ESCAPE NATURAL DISASTERS:
Many Irish immigrants came to America in the 1800s to escape the famine that hit their country. This famine was followed by an epidemic of typhus.

TO FLEE A WARTORN COUNTRY:
When a country goes to war, many families leave to find a safer place to live, such as European Jews did during World War II.

TO GET LAND OF THEIR OWN:
Many countries in Europe were becoming overpopulated and good farmland was getting harder to find. America was still developing and had lots of land.

BY FORCE:
Millions of Africans were brought to America against their will and forced to be slaves. They were unwilling immigrants.

Fan-Fold File of the Journey to America

Materials: index cards (5" by 8"), copier paper, scissors, black markers, glue sticks

With the advent of steamships in the mid-1800s, the journey to America was shortened by several weeks, taking immigrants only five or six days to reach their new home. Discuss different aspects of the immigrants' journeys and fill your classroom library with trade books about the immigrant experience, Ellis Island, Angel Island, and more.

Give each student four large index cards and a sheet of paper. Show students how to create file fans, using the instructions on page 9. On their file fans, have students write about and illustrate the journey of a fictional immigrant. The file fan should include four compartments, each featuring a two-card display. One of the cards should feature a journal entry, and the other an illustration related to the journal entry. The four entries should cover

- the immigrant's country of origin, his or her reason for immigrating to America, and the family members or friends, if any, with whom he or she is traveling
- an important event that happened on the journey
- information about what happened at their port of entry (Ellis Island, Castle Garden, or Angel Island)
- a description of the immigrant's new life in America—where he or she settled, how he or she makes a living, and so on

CREATING THE FAN-FOLD FILE

1. Have students fold a sheet of paper in half widthwise.

2. Ask them to fold it in half again in the same direction.

3. Then have students fold it in half one more time in the same direction.

4. Next, tell students to open up the paper. It should reveal seven creases.

5. Show students how to fan-fold the paper along the creases.

6. Then have them cut the four index cards in half perpendicularly to the lines. This creates eight 4" by 5" index cards.

7. Instruct students to write a journal entry on the lined side of one card and draw a related picture on the blank side of another card, following the criteria found at the bottom of page 8. The illustration should be drawn in black and white to look like an old-fashioned newspaper drawing.

8. Have students glue the first pair of cards to the front of the first fan-fold, the second pair to the second fan-fold, and so on. The final product should look like the example below.

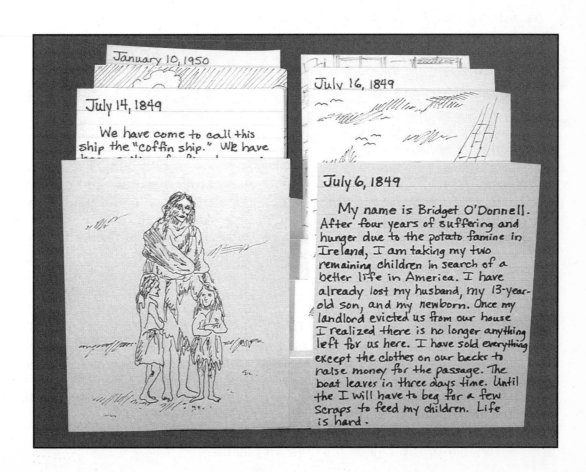

Packing for the Journey

Materials: copies of page 34, construction paper, scissors, glue sticks, colored markers or pencils

Imagine moving to a distant land and having to leave all of your belongings behind. All you can take with you are the clothes on your back and one small suitcase. What few, small possessions would you take? Ask students to put themselves in the place of an immigrant child from the 1800s who had to choose four things to take on the journey. Have students create a flip-flop pop-up book featuring these four items.

CREATING THE FLIP-FLOP POP-UP BOOK

1. Show students how to fold the template vertically so that the lines are on the outside of the fold.

2. Have them cut eight slits along the short dotted lines.

3. Instruct students to refold the paper so that the lines are on the inside. They should gently pull each of the pop-up tabs forward so that each pop-up tab falls into the center. Finally, show them how to make a crease at the base of each tab.

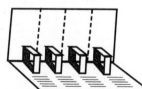

5. Ask students to use a glue stick to glue the outer side of the flip-flop pop-up book to a sheet of construction paper.

6. Next, have students cut along the dashed lines between each pop-up tab to create four flaps.

7. On another sheet of paper, have students draw and cut out four objects that they would pack for the journey to America and then glue these objects to the fronts of the four tabs.

8. Ask students to write the name of each object on the flap above the pop-up tabs and write a paragraph describing the object's importance on the lines below each tab. See the photo above.

9. Ask students to write their name and a title across the covers of the four flaps.

Ancestral Tossed Salad

Materials: copies of pages 35, scissors, colored markers or pencils, construction paper

America is often described as a "melting pot," a place where people from many diverse backgrounds live and blend together to form one unique culture. But perhaps describing America as a "tossed salad" would be more accurate, because each group adds its own unique flavor to the whole.

CREATING THE TOSSED SALAD BULLETIN BOARD

1. Ask students to interview their parents and grandparents to find out where their ancestors came from and to learn the stories of their past.

2. Give each student a copy of the template on page 35 and ask them to write the stories of their ancestors on their lettuce leaves.

3. Have students write on their leaves at varying angles. This way, when you hang the bulletin board, the lettuce leaves can be arranged in different positions.

4. After students have finished writing, ask them to color the leaves light green and cut them out.

5. Hang the students' work on a bulletin board under a banner that reads "Our Class, Like America, Is a Tossed Salad!" Add Walt Whitman's quote as shown in the illustration below.

6. Using colored construction paper, cut out some red tomato slices, yellow pepper wedges, and green cucumbers. Hang these in and around the lettuce leaves to make a tossed salad bulletin board.

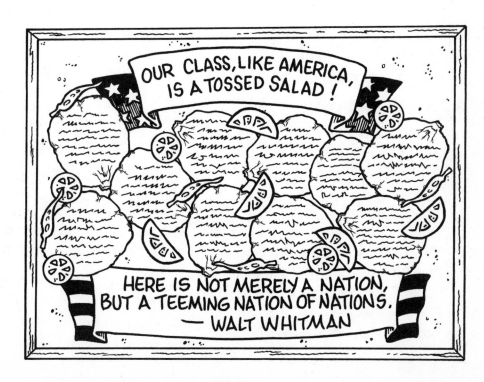

OUR CLASS, LIKE AMERICA, IS A TOSSED SALAD!

HERE IS NOT MERELY A NATION, BUT A TEEMING NATION OF NATIONS. — WALT WHITMAN

A Statue of Symbolism

Materials: white construction paper, colored markers and pencils

The Statue of Liberty, whose original name was *Liberty Enlightening the World*, was one of the first sights many immigrants saw upon their arrival in America. To them, she represented the promise of opportunity. But more important, she was a symbol of freedom—freedom from economic hardships, religious oppression, and tyranny.

The head of Liberty Enlightening the World *on display in a Paris park.*

Discuss symbolism with your students. Explain that there are many hidden symbols in the design of the Statue of Liberty. For example, the seven rays in the statue's crown symbolize the seven seas and seven continents of the world, and the broken chain at her feet symbolizes freedom. Her torch acts as a beacon, symbolizing the idea that enlightenment is the key to achieving freedom. The tablet she holds in her left hand represents a nation based on law, and it is shaped like a keystone—a stone that holds all other stones of a construction in place. The windows in her crown symbolize heaven's rays of light that shine down on the world, and the 13 rows of granite blocks in the statue's base represent the original 13 colonies. Even the direction in which the statue faces is symbolic: It looks toward France, the nation that gave the statue to America as a symbol of the friendship between these two nations.

Discuss other symbols of America with your class—the bald eagle, the Liberty Bell, Uncle Sam, the Stars and Stripes. Ask students to describe what feelings and ideas these images bring to mind. For example, the bald eagle might conjure images of strength, grace, courage, freedom, and majesty.

CREATING THE CLASS FLAG

1. Give students white construction paper and invite them to design a class flag that includes elements of symbolism, such as symbols of school spirit, class members, or educational ideals.

2. Encourage students to carefully consider color choices, form and shape, imagery, and message when designing the flag.

3. After they are finished, ask each student to write a paragraph on the back of the flag describing the symbolism in their design. Invite them to share their paragraphs and flags with the class.

4. Hang the flags around the classroom or in the hallway for all to enjoy.

   You might ask your art teacher to conduct this lesson as a way to integrate the visual arts into your social studies curriculum.

New Colossus Mini-Book

Materials: copies of page 36, scissors, colored markers or pencils

"The New Colossus" is a poem that was written by Emma Lazarus in 1863 and used as a fund-raiser for the Bartholdi Pedestal Fund for the Statue of Liberty. It is an enduring poem that can be found on a bronze plaque at the base of the statue.

CREATING THE MINI-BOOK

1. Give students copies of the template on page 36 and have them fold it according to the instructions on page 8. When folding the mini-book, ask students to make sure that the writing is on the outside and that the pages, once the book is closed, are in sequential order.

2. On each page, have students draw an illustration to accompany the lines of the poem appearing at the bottom of that page. The illustrations should help convey the meaning behind the words of Lazarus's famous poem. Have students write their name on the cover of the mini-book.

As part of the final test on the immigration unit, I have my students memorize and recite Lazarus's poem. Not only is memorization an important skill that students should learn, but this activity exposes them to poetry recitation. I find that having them visualize the pictures they drew helps them with the memorization process. As students prepare to recite the poem, I ask them to concentrate on the eight characteristics of good stage voice and presence, qualities that I enforce throughout the year whenever they speak before the class. These characteristics are:

- *Rate*—the speed at which one speaks
- *Projection*—the volume at which one speaks
- *Clarity*—the ability of the speaker to be understood
- *Expression*—adding variety and feeling to one's speech
- *Pitch*—the highs and lows of a person's speaking voice
- *Stance*—standing straight and tall and confidently when speaking
- *Eye Contact*—looking directly at the audience when speaking
- *Poise*—the ability to recover quickly from a mistake and move on with confidence

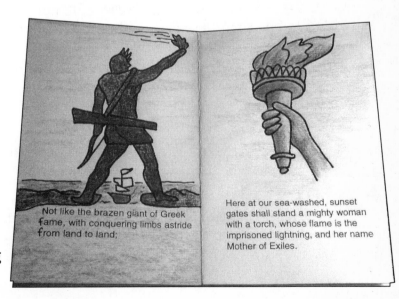

Not like the brazen giant of Greek fame, with conquering limbs astride from land to land;

Here at our sea-washed, sunset gates shall stand a mighty woman with a torch, whose flame is the imprisoned lightning, and her name Mother of Exiles.

Scale Model

Materials: copies of page 37, copier paper, pencils, black markers, tape

Sculptors and artists often make several scale models of their work, increasing the size of each model, before creating the final piece of artwork. Frédéric-Auguste Bartholdi, the French sculptor who designed the Statue of Liberty, not only made several scale drawings of the statue, he made several clay models of it as well. The picture below is one of Bartholdi's working drawings. Your class can explore the concept of scale by using the scale model template to create a nearly 12-foot-tall by 5-foot-wide drawing of the Statue of Liberty.

CREATING THE SCALE MODEL

1. Give each student a copy of the template on page 37 and a few sheets of 8½" by 11" paper.

2. Assign each student three or four coordinates (depending on class size). Be sure that each student has at least one rectangle that includes part of the statue. Have them sketch their rectangles in pencil. Each of these rectangles is smaller than the sheet of paper, so when students sketch the lines/elements of their rectangle to fill the paper, they will automatically increase its scale.

3. Once the drawing on each student's copier paper looks similar to the content of the rectangle on the scale model, have them use a black marker to darken their pencil lines.

4. Ask students to write the coordinates of each rectangle they were assigned on the back of their copy paper.

5. Then, systematically collect the papers and tape them together from behind. While the lines of the large-scale statue might not match up exactly, they will match closely enough to give an impressive version of this famous landmark. Of course, remind your class that this drawing is only 1/46th the size of the real statue.

6. Hang the large class-made model in the hall or gym for everyone to see.

The Great Migration

Materials: copies of page 38, scissors, construction paper, colored markers or pencils, glue sticks

Incorporate mathematics into the study of immigration by having your students create 3D graphs comparing the numbers of immigrants coming to America from different countries during the time of the Great Migration of 1880–1920, which brought 27 million immigrants through Ellis Island.

There are many charts available in books and on the Internet that compare these numbers. Have your students conduct some research to find a graph to reference, or allow them to use the numbers in the chart below.

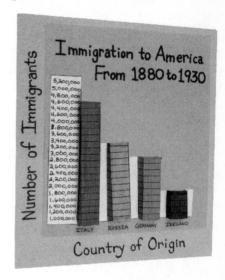

CREATING THE 3D GRAPH

1. Give students copies of the 3D graph template.

2. Ask them to write the numbers of immigrants they are comparing in the left-hand column of the graph (similar to the example in the photograph above).

3. Then have students choose four groups of immigrants to compare. Have them write the countries of origin of these four groups across the bottom of the graph. (You might want to have students work in groups so that they can create several graphs comparing even more population groups.)

4. Ask students to shade the columns with markers or colored pencils up to the appropriate graph line and cut out the graph.

5. Instruct them to cut away the unshaded top of each column and then carefully fold the graph so that the columns stand out from the gray strips. A side view of the folded paper should look like this.

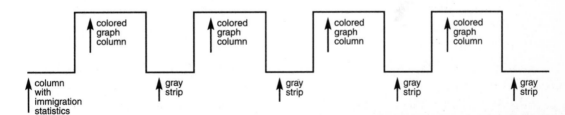

6. Have students use a glue stick to attach the gray strips to a piece of light-colored construction paper.

7. They should add headings down the left side and bottom of the graph to explain what the numbers and columns represent.

8. Finally, ask them to add a title and their name to the 3D graph.

Immigration from 1880–1930	
ITALY	4,600,000
AUSTRO-HUNGARY	4,000,000
RUSSIA	3,300,000
GERMANY	2,800,000
BRITAIN	2,300,000
CANADA	2,300,000
IRELAND	1,700,000
SWEDEN	1,100,000

Ellis Island Web Pages

Materials: copies of home pages from the Internet, trade books about Ellis Island, yarn, 4' sheets of bulletin board paper, glue, colored markers and pencils, yarn

Print out several examples of home pages from the Internet, such as www.usmint.gov, www.mothergoose.com, or www.scholastic.com. Share them with your class and discuss the pros and cons of the different layouts and designs. Point out the way the Web master used buttons and navigational tools to make it easy for viewers to find their way around the Web site.

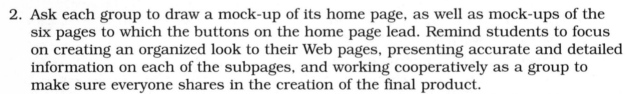

CREATING THE WEB PAGES

1. Divide students into small groups and have each group design a Web site that focuses on Ellis Island. Ask groups to brainstorm the types of information that could be included on the home page and come up with a design. The home page should feature six buttons that lead to additional pages. These buttons might lead to topics such as History, Construction of the Buildings, Processing Immigrants, People Who Worked at Ellis Island, the Decline of the Island, Creating the Museum, among others.

2. Ask each group to draw a mock-up of its home page, as well as mock-ups of the six pages to which the buttons on the home page lead. Remind students to focus on creating an organized look to their Web pages, presenting accurate and detailed information on each of the subpages, and working cooperatively as a group to make sure everyone shares in the creation of the final product.

3. Stress that part of their final grade will be determined by how well they share in the production of the poster. All group members should proofread everything on the poster, regardless of who created each element, because spelling will count as part of their final grade.

4. Give each group a large strip of bulletin board paper. (I use a different color paper for each group.) Ask students to put their home page in the center of the sheet and label it Home Page. Have them surround the home page with the six additional pages.

5. Ask them to glue a length of yarn leading from the button on the home page to its related subpage.

6. Encourage students to use creative lettering to add a title to their poster, making sure to include each group member's name.

7. Hang the completed posters in the hall so that other classes can learn more about Ellis Island.

Wallet Photos of Ellis Island

Materials: copies of pages 39 and 40, scissors, tape

By studying historical photographs, students learn about the history of Ellis Island from its earliest days as an immigration station to the restored immigration museum that it is today.

CREATING THE WALLET PHOTOS

1. Make back-to-back copies of the templates on pages 39 and 40 so that the writing appears upside down on the back of the pictures.

2. Give students copies of the templates and have them cut along the vertical line between the photographs.

3. Then ask students to tape the photos into one long column, with "The Journey Over" at the top and the question under "The Ellis Island Immigration Museum" at the bottom.

4. Have them fold the bottom edge of this column upward so that it aligns with the thin line above the title "The Ellis Island Immigration Museum." Instruct them to crease along this fold.

5. Students should continue to fold the paper upward a total of five times until they reach the top. Then the photos will flip out when the student holds the top photo.

As the photos flip out, a question will be revealed on the panel opposite each photo. Conduct a whole-class discussion about each of these questions, and have students record their responses in the appropriate area. (A list of suggested responses can be found on page 18.)

After students have answered the questions, they should write their name on the cover of their wallet photos and create a title, such as "Tamyra's Wallet Photos of Ellis Island." They should also draw a related illustration on the cover.

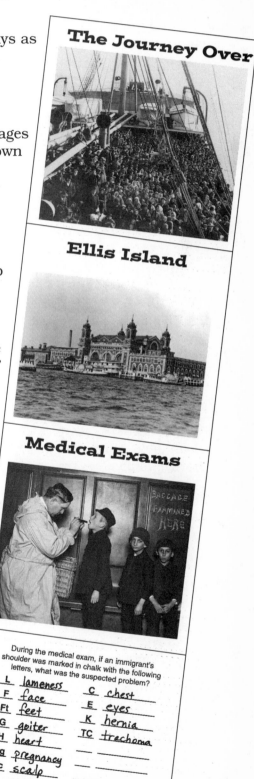

The Journey Over

Ellis Island

Medical Exams

During the medical exam, if an immigrant's shoulder was marked in chalk with the following letters, what was the suspected problem?

L lameness   C chest
F face   E eyes
Ft feet   K hernia
G goiter   TC trachoma
H heart
Pg pregnancy
Sc scalp
X mental

Suggested Answers for Wallet Photos

THE JOURNEY OVER:
Describe the hardships and potential dangers that immigrants faced on their journey over.

Because of the close quarters, epidemics could spread quickly across the ship. Cooking fires sometimes spread and burned the ship. Shipwrecks and storms killed hundreds of immigrants. The days were long and very boring. Immigrants had to sleep on hard cots in cramped conditions.

ELLIS ISLAND:
Create a brief time line of Ellis Island's history.

1620s—Dutch name it Oyster Island after the oyster beds they find there.

1808—United States buys Ellis Island from New York for $10,000; named after former owner.

1892—The immigration station is opened on January 1.

1897—Fire destroys the original wooden buildings on Ellis Island.

1900—The Ellis Island Immigration Station reopens with brick and ironwork structures.

1907—On a record day, 11,747 immigrants pass through Ellis Island.

1954—Ellis Island is officially closed; more than 12 million immigrants had passed through since 1892.

1990—The Ellis Island Immigration Museum opens on September 10.

MEDICAL EXAMS:
During the medical exam, if an immigrant's shoulder was marked in chalk with the following letters, what was the suspected problem?

L	lameness
F	face
Ft	feet
G	goiter
H	heart
Pg	pregnancy
Sc	scalp
X	mental problems, feeblemindedness
C	chest or tuberculosis
E	eyes
K	hernia
TC	trachoma

LEGAL EXAMS:
What information did an immigrant have to provide during a legal exam?

Immigrants had to provide their name, age, sex, marital status, nationality, occupation, last residence, point of departure, destination, who paid for the voyage, how much money they had, criminal record, the names of any relatives in the United States, and whether or not they had a job waiting in the United States.

THE ELLIS ISLAND IMMIGRATION MUSEUM:
Do you think the United States should limit the number of immigrants allowed to enter the country each year? Why or why not?

Answers may vary. Encourage students to consider all sides of the issue.

Famous Immigrants People Books

Materials: white construction paper, craft materials, scissors, glue sticks, colored markers or pencils

Immigrants played an important role in the changing face of our country. In addition to each group bringing cultural differences with them, many immigrants went on to become famous Americans in their own right.

Your class can learn about these famous Americans who were once immigrants by creating people books following the directions on page 20. Use the list below as a starting point and add additional names if you like. Assign a different name to each student, and have students use trade books, textbooks, and the Internet to find out as much as possible about the person assigned to them. After they create their people books, have students give oral presentations about these immigrants' accomplishments.

Once students have completed their presentations, staple the arms and legs of the people books to a bulletin board. Add a banner that reads "Famous American Immigrants."

Famous Immigrants

Jane Addams	Marcus Garvey	Zubin Mehta
Madeleine Albright	Kahlil Gibran	Hakeem Olajuwon
Charles Atlas	Arshile Gorky	Hyman G. Rickover
Mikhail Baryshnikov	Bob Hope	Edward G. Robinson
Claudette Colbert	Sol Hurok	Knute Rockne
Xavier Cugat	Al Jolson	Arthur Rubinstein
Karl Dane	Elia Kazan	Lee Strasberg
Father Edward	Ruby Keeler	Rudolph Valentino
Irving Frank	Henry Kissinger	Baron von Trapp & family
Felix Frankfurter	Bela Lugosi	An Wang

FEMALES:

1. Ask students to fold a sheet of white construction paper in half twice horizontally and then once vertically.

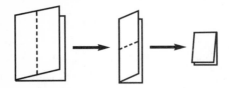

2. Have them open it up to reveal eight panels.

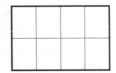

3. Instruct students to cut the bottom left and bottom right panels along the dotted lines, as shown. Have them save the two scraps of paper.

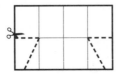

4. Next, have students fold in the top left and top right panels.

5. Then ask students to glue the two scraps that were cut away behind the top two panels, as shown.

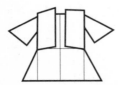

6. Have students add a head, legs, and hands to the figure.

7. Tell students to use buttons, markers, fabrics, dimensional glue, and other craft materials to decorate the figure. They can create clothing that is representative of the historical figure.

8. Using construction paper, students should create an object to put in the figure's hand that is relevant to her accomplishment.

9. Ask students to write—inside the two flaps—two complete, detailed paragraphs describing the significance and the accomplishments of the immigrant on whom they are reporting.

10. Finally, have students prepare an oral report on this person to give to the class.

MALES:

To create male people books, simply cut the bottom left and bottom right panels as indicated below, and make a slit up the center to create pants. Glue the two scraps of paper that were cut away behind the top two panels to create sleeves. Then follow steps 6 through 10 above.

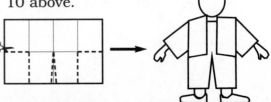

Native Costumes

Materials: copies of page 41, oak tag or poster board, scissors, craft materials, construction paper, colored pencils or markers

Students can learn a lot about the diversity of immigrants who settled in America during the late 1800s by studying the native costumes of their cultures. Ask each student to pick a different immigrant group. (Some students may choose the same group.) Have students research the ways men and women from that nation dressed in the late 1800s and create two paper dolls featuring traditional clothing from that period.

Give students copies of the template on page 41 and have them cut out the figures. Ask them to trace the edges of the paper dolls onto a sheet of oak tag or poster board and cut out the figures again. (Students can also share the paper templates if you prefer.) Have students use construction paper and craft materials to dress the paper dolls in traditional costumes, as a man and woman from the culture they chose would have dressed in the late 1800s.

In the box below the figures, have students write the name of the culture represented and a paragraph describing the native costumes that they created.

Finally, have the students fold the paper dolls in half (like a book) so their faces meet. When they are reopened, the paper dolls will stand freely. Display everyone's paper dolls on a table or counter and enjoy the diverse costumes of the cultures that made America what it is today!

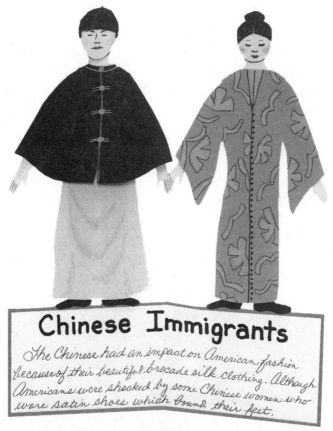

Chinese Immigrants

The Chinese had an impact on American fashion because of their beautiful brocade silk clothing. Although Americans were shocked by some Chinese women who wore satin shoes which bound their feet.

You Are What You Eat

Materials: copies of page 42, scissors, cookbooks, paper plates, craft materials, construction paper, colored markers or pencils

Spice up your unit by asking students to research traditional foods and distinctive dishes that were introduced to this country by the many immigrant groups that settled here. Jewish immigrants introduced lox and bagels and potato latkes, Germans brought bratwurst and liverwurst, Poles contributed kielbasa and pierogis, Russians introduced chicken Kiev and Stroganoff. American menus these days feature a buffet of cultural contributions—Mexican, French, Chinese, Italian, Japanese, Cajun, Indian, Greek, and Vietnamese, among many others.

CREATING THE FLAVORS OF THE WORLD BULLETIN BOARD

1. Gather a wide variety of cookbooks from the library that feature the recipes of different countries. (Consider asking students to bring in cookbooks from home as well.)

2. Ask students to choose a typical dish from one country. Have them copy the recipe neatly on a separate sheet of paper.

3. Then instruct them to write a paragraph on the napkin template describing the final dish—its taste, look, smell, and appeal.

4. Next, ask students to use a paper plate, craft materials, and construction paper to create a 3D replica of the finished dish. Students might curl spaghetti noodles using strands of yellow construction paper and scissors, sprinkle red pepper across their dish using spray glue and red confetti, or create sausages using rolled tubes of brown construction paper.

5. Display the plates on a bulletin board. Hang the recipe for each dish next to its corresponding paper plate.

6. Have your students cut out the fork from the template and color it. Then have them cut out their paragraphs and fold them diagonally like a napkin. Staple or tape the back of the napkins next to each dish and then glue the forks onto the the front of napkins.

7. As a culminating culinary activity, ask parents to use the recipes to cook the actual dishes. Have students bring the food to class and then hold a sampling party for students to try the cuisines that give our country its unique international flavor.

22

The Origins of Festivities in America

Materials: 8½" by 11" copy paper, ribbon or yarn, oak tag or poster board, scissors, one bead for each student with a hole large enough to hold doubled ribbon, colored markers or pencils, glue sticks

When immigrants from around the world settled in America, they brought their holidays and celebrations with them. Over time, these festivities became a part of the American landscape, and today many Americans take part in these celebrations without understanding their true origins.

Have students research the origins of contemporary holidays to create a decorative display of ornament books to brighten your classroom. Suggested topics for your students to explore include Cinco de Mayo, piñatas, Kwanzaa, Shichi-Go-San, Christmas, Christmas trees, St. Nicholas, Mardi Gras, Rosh Hashanah, Hanukkah, St. Patrick's Day, and the Chinese New Year. (In fact, many ethnic groups have their own New Year celebrations and dates.)

CREATING THE ORNAMENT BOOK

1. Give each student three sheets of copy paper.

2. Direct students to fold the top left corner of one sheet down diagonally to the right so that the top edge of the paper aligns with the right edge of the paper. Crease along the fold.

3. Have students cut off the bottom strip of paper to create an 8½" square.

4. Ask students to fold the square in half vertically and crease it. Have them open it and then fold it in half horizontally, creasing it again. When opened, the paper will have three creases (as shown at right).

5. Direct students to repeat these steps for the other two pieces of paper.

6. Have students place the paper in front of them so that a corner is pointing down, making sure one of the diamond shapes is at the bottom.

CONTINUED ON PAGE 24

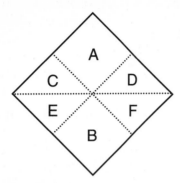

7. In the top diamond on each page (section A in the diagram above), have students use creative lettering to write the name of a holiday, festivity, or celebratory element that originated in another country. Have students report on a different holiday on each of their three pages.

8. In the bottom diamond on each page (section B), ask students to draw and color an illustration of the festivity named in section A.

9. In the top left triangle on each page (section C), have students write a few complete sentences about the country in which the festivity originated.

10. In the top right triangle on each page (section D), ask students to write a couple of sentences describing the nature of the festivity and why it began.

11. In the bottom left triangle on each page (section E), ask students to describe the time of year in which the festivity takes place and explain why this date was chosen.

12. In the bottom right triangle on each page (section F), have students write a list of interesting facts they learned about the festivity.

13. Each page of the ornament book should now look something like the illustration above.

14. Instruct students to use colored pencils to color the twelve triangular shapes on the back side of the paper.

15. Then have students fold all three pages in half along the diagonal crease so that the writing is on the inside.

16. Direct students to push points A and B into the inside to point C, making a smaller square.

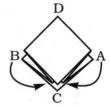

17. Ask students to glue the back of section B of page 1 to the back of section A of page 2, making sure to line up point D on both pages.

18. Then have students glue the back of section B of page 2 to the back of section B of page 3, making sure to line up point D on both pages.

CONTINUED ON PAGE 25

19. Have students glue a 36" ribbon around the stack of pages along the C-D line on both sides, leaving tails of equal lengths hanging from point C.

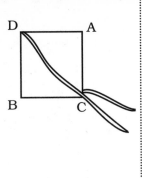

20. Students should cut two 4¼" squares from the card stock and glue one piece to each side of the stack of pages, covering the ribbons.

21. Then they can thread both ends of the ribbon through the bead. Have them tie the ends of the ribbons with a couple of knots to prevent the bead from sliding off.

22. To open the ornament book, slide the bead up to the knot and open the pages so that the covers meet. Slide the bead down to lock the book into place.

23. To display the ornament books, hang a string across your classroom. Tie varying lengths of thread from the string. Tie a paper clip to the end of each piece of thread and hang the ornament books from the paper clips. When a breeze blows past the ornament books, they spin and create a dazzling display to jazz up the classroom.

An Immigrant's Treasures

Materials: copies of page 43, construction paper, scissors, glue sticks, envelopes, craft materials, colored markers or pencils, binding machine or hole punch and yarn

Students will explore the struggles of an immigrant child by creating a scrapbook that holds the memories of his or her past, arduous journey, and life in America.

You can use this idea as a unit-long activity by asking your students to create elements to include in the scrapbook as they learn about them in class. Or you can assign it as a culminating activity or group project at the end of your unit.

Give each student five large sheets of construction paper. Have them bind the sheets together along one side using a binding machine or a hole punch and yarn.

Ask students to put themselves in the shoes of an immigrant child their age who came to America in the late 1800s or early 1900s. Then instruct students to create a scrapbook that reflects the thoughts, feelings, and experiences of this child. The scrapbook should include the following elements:

SCRAPBOOK COVER—The scrapbook cover should include the immigrant's name, the student's name, and an illustration. The illustration can be a "photo" of the immigrant, a landmark or image from the immigrant's country of origin, an American symbol, or some other image of the student's choice.

FAMILY PHOTO—Ask students to draw a large "photograph" of the immigrant's family. Have students use a No. 2 pencil to simulate the black and white photography of the day. Ask students to write a list of the vital statistics of each family member (name, age, and occupation) next to the photograph.

DIARY ENTRY—Have students write a diary entry that describes the immigrant's feelings on the night before his or her journey to America. It should be written in the first person and include the reason the family is emigrating from their homeland, the "date" on which the diary entry was written, and information about the diarist.

PICTURES AND PHOTOGRAPHS—Four pictures or photographs should be scattered throughout the scrapbook. Students can use the template on page 43 to create the photographs. A complete sentence should be written that describes each of the photos. The four pictures should illustrate the following:
- a major landmark or sight from the immigrant's country of origin
- the most difficult part of the immigrant's journey on the ship to America
- an event that happened to the immigrant at Ellis Island
- a scene from the immigrant's life in America

LETTER TO A FRIEND—Instruct students to write a letter from the immigrant child to a friend in his or her homeland. The letter should describe the immigrant's emotions when he or she first saw America, the family's housing situation, where the parents work, where he or she goes to school or works, any challenges they face, how life is different in the new country, and so forth. Ask students to put the letter in an envelope, address it, and tape it into the scrapbook.

INSPECTION PAPERS—Ask students to create a document issued to the immigrant at Ellis Island and tape it into the scrapbook. This document should include the immigrant's name, age, sex, occupation, marital status, nationality, last residence, point of departure, destination, date of departure, and date of arrival. The document could be in the form of a mini-book, following the instructions on page 8.

SOUVENIRS AND MEMENTOS—Have students create, collect, or find at least six souvenirs that the immigrant child would have put into the scrapbook. These objects should reflect events in the child's life and journey.

Culminating Activity

At the end of your immigration unit, set up a mock Ellis Island in your gymnasium for the students to pass through. Divide your students into families of one to four members—single students can represent immigrants traveling alone, larger groups can represent parents with children or extended families. When they enter the gym, give each student a tag with a number on it. Once their number is called, students will make their way through different stations, each of which is supervised by an adult.

At the first station students will be given a basic interview. If possible, have a foreign-language-speaking parent ask the students questions in different languages. Have a second parent write the answers on the student's tag. Instruct parents to "Americanize" any difficult names or make them simpler to pronounce.

Then have students proceed to the health check station, where their heads and nails will be examined for lice and favus. The "doctor" will ask students their names to see if they can hear and speak. If the doctor finds a medical problem, he will write the appropriate letter in chalk on the student's shoulder. (See the list of potential medical problems and their corresponding symbols on page 18.) If students have a chalk mark and the sickness is curable, they will be detained and sent to the hospital until they are better. If the disease is contagious and/or incurable, they will be sent to a special hospital until a boat can take them back to their native counties.

Students then proceed to other stations—following directions, identification cards, and vision screening. At each station, the supervising adult should mark on the student's tag if the student had difficulties with the required activities or seemed confused.

After all stations are completed, check each student and decide if he or she can immigrate. Some students should easily immigrate, while others should be sent before a review board or deported. After the activity, have students discuss their feelings during their immigration process.

Finally, allow students to play games that originated outside of the United States, such as soccer or lawn bowling. They can also partake of special ethnic foods that students, parents, and teachers prepare or bring.

Readers Theater:
The West Wind Carries My Thoughts

Materials: copies of pages 44–48

Nothing taps into the multiple intelligences of your class more than creative dramatics. It gets the kinesthetic learners up on their feet, provides the interpersonal learners with the chance to relate to others, offers the aural learners the opportunity to hear a story unfold, and provides linguistic learners with a forum for speaking in front of an audience. By having students respond through writing and artistic follow-up activities, you'll tap into all of the language arts—reading, writing, speaking, and listening.

Reading plays aloud can also provide students with opportunities to make connections between history and their own lives. Taking on a role, even for a short time, allows learners to become part of our history, to become emotionally involved in the stories of other people, and to explore choices and lives foreign from their own.

Give each student a copy of *The West Wind Carries My Thoughts*, a play about Angel Island by Sarah J. Glasscock, and have students read it aloud. Consider having students perform the play for other classes or turn it into a radio play, complete with sound effects and music. After the class reads the play, you may want to use the following activities to extend students' understanding of the Angel Island experience and the immigration movement in general.

PANNING FOR GOLD AND WORKING ON THE RAILROAD
Chinese laborers made an impact in the goldfields of California and on the Central Pacific Railroad. Challenge students to research the California gold rush of 1848 or the completion of the transcontinental railroad in 1869 to learn about the contribution of other immigrant groups to each event. Encourage them to seek folk songs, poetry, or short stories by writers such as Bret Harte, or nonfiction by Mark Twain written about the gold rush or the railroad. Compare and contrast these works with passages about the same time periods from *China Men* by Maxine Hong Kingston.

CLOSING THE DOOR ON THE CHINESE
Numerous laws were enacted to keep Chinese immigrants from enjoying the full benefits of American life. These included California state laws such as the Foreign Miner's Tax in 1853 and the Immigrant Tax in 1855. The federal government enacted the Burlingame Treaty in 1868, which encouraged Chinese migration but prohibited their naturalization, and the Chinese Exclusion Act of 1882, which shut the door on Chine immigrants. Guide students in tracking down laws and ordinances that directly affected Chinese immigrants. Compile their findings and discuss the effects of each law and ordinance.

SAVING ANGEL ISLAND
In the early 1970s, when buildings at Angel Island were schedule for demolition, a park ranger discovered poems written by the Chinese immigrants. Direct students to investigate the history of Angel Island, from its beginnings to its designation as a National Historic Landmark. Encourage them to write poems describing its history. If the book *Island: Poetry and History of Chinese Immigrants on Angel Island, 1910–1940* by Mark Him Lai, Genny Lim, and Judy Yung (Seattle: University of Washington Press, 1991) is available, let each student choose a poem. Hold a seminar on Angel Island for other classes in your school, sharing its history and reading aloud its poetry.

Immigration Study Guide

Create a wonderful study guide for students by having them compile all the mini-books, activities, and projects into an interactive immigration "textbook." Over the course of the unit, ask students to save all of their papers and projects in a pocket folder. At the end of the unit, use a binding machine to put them all together. If you don't have access to one, use a hole punch and yarn. Here are suggestions for compiling each page.

Materials: all of the projects students have created, 8½" by 11" paper, tape, glue sticks, binding machine (if available) or hole punch and yarn

COVER

When binding the notebooks, add a page of heavy stock to the front and back. Have students use creative lettering to add a title to their notebook and then draw a total of ten icons around the front and back covers. The icons can represent any ten things learned over the course of the unit. Ask students to number the icons and, on the inside front cover, write a complete sentence describing the relevance of each icon.

PAGE 1

Students can create a pocket-page to hold their SEVEN REASONS FOR IMMIGRATION MINI-BOOK by folding a piece of 8½" by 11" paper in half horizontally, slipping another sheet of paper into the fold, and taping the edges. Encourage students to add a title and decorate the page.

PAGE 2

Students can create another pocket-page to hold their FAN-FOLD FILE, which can be squeezed together and inserted into the pocket.

PAGE 3

Have students glue their FLIP-FLOP POP-UP BOOK sideways on this page. The flaps can simply be lifted to reveal the information inside.

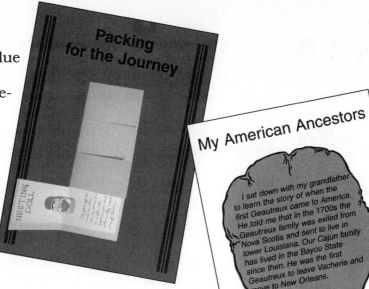

PAGE 4

Have students glue their ANCESTRAL TOSSED SALAD lettuce leaf onto a sheet of paper to bind into their interactive notebooks.

PAGE 5

Bind the students' class flag into the notebook as page 5. If the flag is larger than the page, turn the flag sideways, bind in the shorter edge, and then fold the flag inward; it can then be opened to reveal the full flag.

PAGE 6

Ask students to glue the back of the NEW COLOSSUS MINI-BOOK onto this page. They can add a decorative border to the page.

PAGE 7

Ask students to draw a 2D version of their GREAT MIGRATION 3D GRAPH on a copy of the template (found on page 38). Bind this graph into the notebook.

PAGE 8

Have students glue the back of panel two of their WALLET PHOTOS OF ELLIS ISLAND to this page. The "wallet" can be opened to reveal the photos inside.

PAGE 9

Have students glue the back of their PEOPLE BOOK to this page. The arms can then be folded across the figure's chest, allowing the interactive notebook to close.

PAGE 10

Students can glue the back of the right-hand NATIVE COSTUMES PAPER DOLL to page 10. The left-hand doll can then be "closed" like a book.

PAGE 11

Bind their YOU ARE WHAT YOU EAT recipe into the notebook for page 11.

PAGE 12

Ask students to create a pocket-page into which they can insert their closed ornament book of FESTIVITIES IN AMERICA.

Vocabulary Immigrant Template

WORD:
DEFINITION:

WORD:
DEFINITION:

Vocabulary Immigrant Template

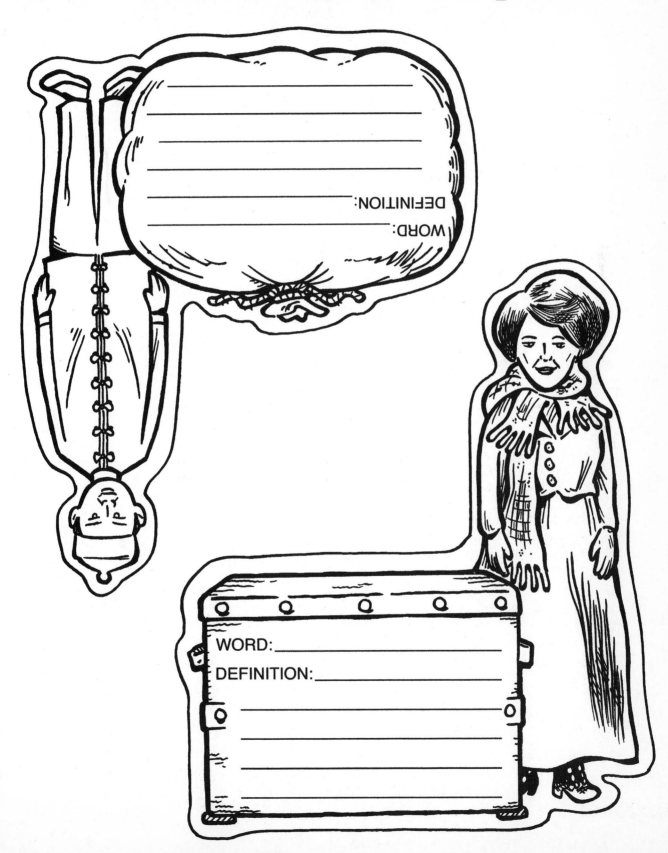

WORD:

DEFINITION:

WORD: _____

DEFINITION: _____

_____

_____

_____

Tossed Salad Template

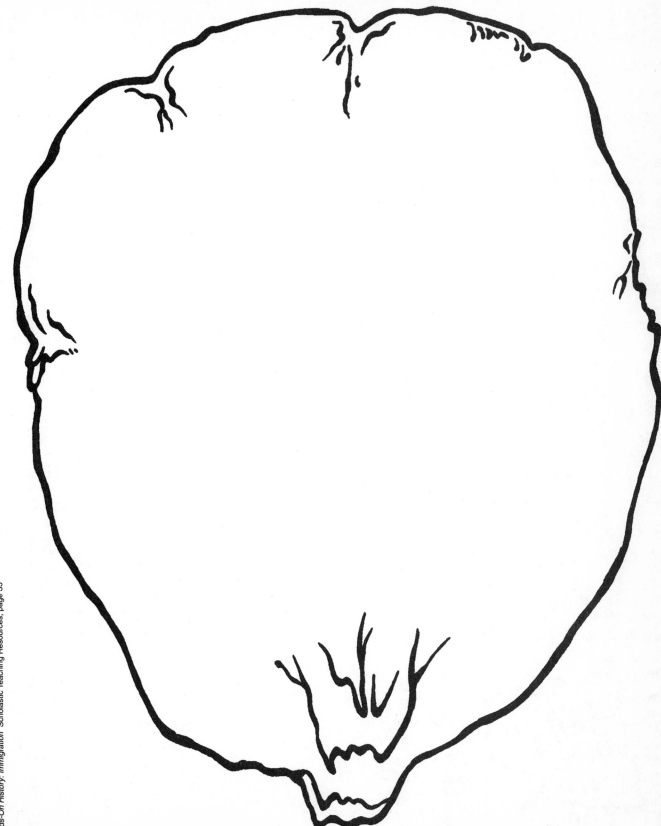

The New Colossus

by Emma Lazarus

Not like the brazen giant of Greek fame, with conquering limbs astride from land to land;

Here at our sea-washed, sunset gates shall stand a mighty woman with a torch, whose flame is the imprisoned lightning, and her name Mother of Exiles.

From her beacon-hand glows world-wide welcome; her mild eyes command the air-bridged harbor that twin cities frame.

"Keep, ancient lands, your storied pomp!" cries she with silent lips.

"Give me your tired, your poor, your huddled masses yearning to breathe free, the wretched refuse of your teeming shore.

Send these, the homeless, tempest-tossed to me. I lift my lamp beside the golden door."

Scale Model Template

A B C D E F G H I J K L M

1 2 3 4 5 6 7

The Great Migration 3D Graph Template

Write the numbers representing the groups of immigrants you are comparing in this shaded column.

- Use colored pencils or markers to shade in the columns for the populations you are comparing.
- Cut out the graph and fold it into a 3D graph following your teacher's instructions.
- Glue the 3D graph onto a sheet of construction paper.
- Add the proper headings along the left side and the bottom of the graph.
- Add a title to your graph.

The Journey Over

Legal Exams

Ellis Island

The Ellis Island Immigration Museum

Medical Exams

Do you think the United States should limit the number of immigrants allowed to enter the country each year? Why or why not?

_____

_____

_____

_____

_____

_____

_____

_____

Describe the hardships and potential dangers that immigrants faced on their journey over.

_____

_____

_____

_____

_____

_____

_____

What information did an immigrant have to provide during a legal exam?

_____

_____

_____

_____

_____

_____

_____

During the medical exam, if an immigrant's shoulder was marked in chalk with the following letters, what was the suspected problem?

L	_____	**C**	_____
F	_____	**E**	_____
Ft	_____	**K**	_____
G	_____	**TC**	_____
H	_____	___	_____
Pg	_____	___	_____
Sc	_____	___	_____
X	_____	___	_____

Create a brief time line of Ellis Island's history.

Date	**Event**
_____	_____
_____	_____
_____	_____
_____	_____
_____	_____
_____	_____
_____	_____

Native Costumes--Paper Doll Template

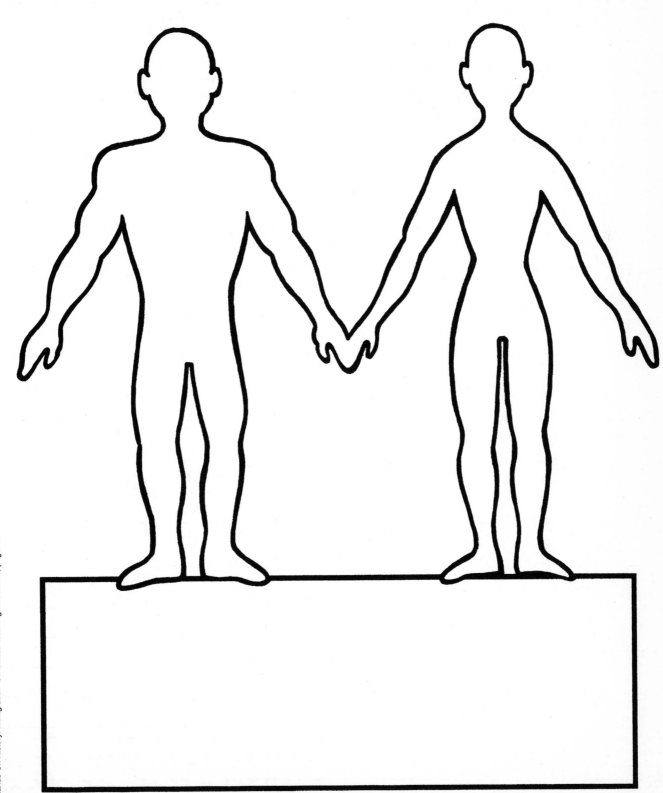

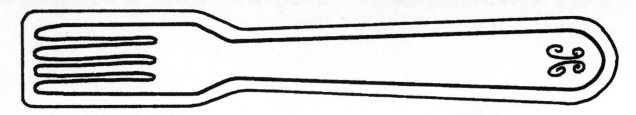

You Are What You Eat

_____

_____

_____

_____

_____

_____

_____

_____

_____

_____

_____

Snapshot Template

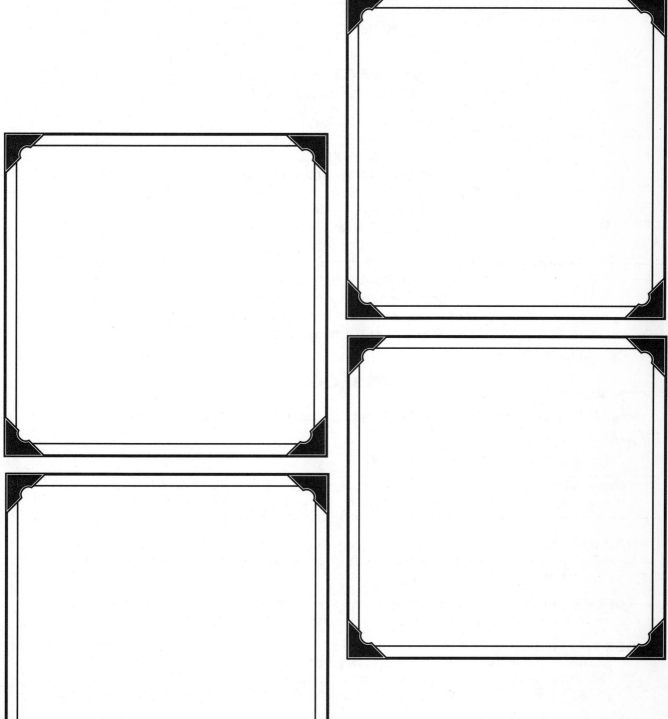

The West Wind Carries My Thoughts

by Sarah J. Glasscock

Cast of Characters
(in order of appearance)

Roy Ng: Guide at Angel Island Immigration Station
Tina Chu: Sixth-grade girl visiting Angel Island Immigration Station
Paul Chu: Tina's father
Maxine Chu: Tina's mother
Yung Lin: Gold prospector; Paul's great-grandfather
Beau Saunders: Gold prospector
Louis Fabre: Storekeeper
Tom Lo: Merchant
Sammy Lo (Yik Sem): Tom Lo's "paper son"; Maxine's grandfather
Chin Li Chu: Paul's grandmother
Lois Wong: Chinese immigrant
Inspector Barnett: Immigration official
Wei Shee: Chinese immigrant

PROLOGUE

Scene: Present day, Angel Island Immigration Station in San Francisco.

ROY NG: Welcome to the Angel Island Immigration Station. My name is Roy Ng. Is this your first visit to Angel Island?

TINA CHU: Yes, but my great-grandmother Chin Li was here for a long time. We want to find the poem she wrote. Sammy Lo, my great-grandfather on my other side, was here, too, but we don't know if he wrote a poem or not. He never said.

ROY NG: Most of the poems are unsigned. Some of them have been destroyed over the years. It may not be possible to find your great-grandmother's poem, but let's see what we can do.

TINA CHU: I know the poem. She used to recite it to my father. He wrote it down in Chinese and in English. I'll know it when I see it.

ROY NG: Well, let's get started on our tour, then. I'll just tell you about Angel Island as we walk. From the years 1910 through 1940, over one million Asian immigrants came here to Angel Island. Some stayed for days. Some stayed for weeks or months. Some even stayed here for years. Sadly, some were sent back.

PAUL CHU: What happened before then? My great-granddad came here during the gold rush. My dad says he thinks it was maybe around the 1850s or 1860s. Something like that.

ROY NG: Until the year 1882, Chinese could come to the United States, provided they could scrape together the money for their passage. The gold rush brought the first big wave of Chinese to the United States. A family might mortgage their land to buy a ticket for a son to come to America. Many hoped to stay here for a few years, just long enough to make some money, and then return to China. Most stayed, though.

PAUL CHU: Yung Lin, my great-great-granddad, stayed. He came here searching for *Gum Shan*, the Gold Mountain, and he found it. He went back to China only to marry and bring his wife back with him. They were able to get back into the United States without any trouble. But Chin Li—my grandmother—when my granddad brought her from China, she was held here for six months.

MAXINE CHU: I still think it's so strange that your grandmother and my grandfather were here at Angel Island at the same time.

TINA CHU: But they didn't know yet that you both would be born and meet and get married, and that they would be related.

MAXINE CHU: That's true. My grandfather was having a hard enough time trying to keep his new name and his new history straight. He was a paper son. A merchant sponsored him.

TINA CHU: Do you want to hear their stories, Mr. Ng?

ACT 1: In Search of Gum Shan

Scene 1: 1858, at a gold-mining claim a few miles outside of Marysville, California.

YUNG LIN: How long have you worked the claim?

BEAU SAUNDERS: Long enough to know that either I'm no prospector or I'm just plain unlucky.

YUNG LIN: The price seems high.

BEAU SAUNDERS (*quickly*): Because I haven't overworked it. There's gold there, I'm sure of it. As sure as I am that I'm not cut out for this kind of work. I just want to make enough money to get back home to Indiana. This is Gum Shan, all right. This is Gold Mountain.

YUNG LIN: How about the other miners in the area? Are there many?

BEAU SAUNDERS: They all pretty much keep to themselves. You might get into trouble in Marysville if you walk by the wrong man. You might get your pigtail pulled there.

YUNG LIN: By law in China we must wear our hair like this.

BEAU SAUNDERS: Some people might tell you that this isn't China.

YUNG LIN: Like you, we're going back home one day. So we keep our "pigtails."

BEAU SAUNDERS: Tell you what—you pay me for this claim, and you can keep your pigtail and all the gold you find.

Scene 2: 1859, in the Marysville general store.

LOUIS FABRE: The word is you're finding a lot of gold on Beau Saunders's old claim.

YUNG LIN: A little gold.

LOUIS FABRE: The word is you're using some kind of new mining techniques out there. Waterwheels or some such thing.

YUNG LIN: Old mining techniques in China. May I have five pounds of sugar, please?

LOUIS FABRE: If you have as much gold dust as I hear you have, you can have anything in this store.

YUNG LIN: Just five pounds of sugar, please.

LOUIS FABRE (*laughing and shaking his head*): You Celestials, you sure play your hands close to your chests. Is that all I'm going to get out of you? A little gold, old mining techniques, five pounds sugar. Don't you get lonely, being so far from home? What about your family? How long has it been since you've seen your relatives? You might even have a wife and children waiting back in China for you to come back a rich man. It must be hard, but I guess life's got to be pretty poor back there.

YUNG LIN: How much for the sugar?

LOUIS FABRE: I hope for your sake that you're married. I don't think I've ever seen a Chinese woman in this country. If you plan on staying here, I don't know how you'll ever find yourself a Chinese woman for a wife.

YUNG LIN: The best place to find a Chinese woman is in China. How much for the sugar?

LOUIS FABRE: Say, did you see the new dime novels that just came in? Best way in the world to enlarge your English vocabulary. I don't imagine you get much company out there on your claim.

ACT 2: "Paper Sons" and Real Wives

Scene 1: 1915, on board the steamship *Liberty* headed for San Francisco. Tom Lo and his "paper son" Sammy Lo are standing at the ship's rail. Tom is testing Sammy.

TOM LO: What is your name?

SAMMY LO: Sammy Lo.

TOM LO: How many outside doors does your house in China have?

SAMMY LO: Two outside doors—one small and one large.

TOM LO: Who lives in the second house in your row?

SAMMY LO: Second house in my row? (*thinking*) Leon Gai.

TOM LO: You can't stop and think. You have to *know*. Tell me about Leon Gai's wife.

SAMMY LO: Her name is Gong Shee. She has bound feet.

TOM LO: Do they have any children?

SAMMY LO: Two sons.

TOM LO: Who lives in the third house in the first row in your village?

SAMMY LO: Third house, first row . . . is . . . Yi Chun Yau.

TOM LO: No. There is no Yi Chun Yau in my village.

SAMMY LO (*miserably*)**:** I forgot. He lives in my village.

TOM LO: You have to forget who you are and where you came from. Remember only this: You are my son, born in my village. You're a student. Once you convince the *luk yi*—the greenclothes men—that you are my son and they let you into America, then you can go back to being who you really are.

SAMMY LO: I don't like lying.

TOM LO: Neither do I, but what choice do we have? The Chinese Exclusion Act says no Chinese workers can come into America. Merchants are okay. Students are okay. I've lived in America for 25 years. I'm a merchant. Before, if I tried to visit my family in China and come back to the United States, luk yi looked at me and said, "Maybe you are a merchant and maybe you aren't." There was no guarantee that they would let me back in. Then the earthquake hit. All the birth records in San Francisco went up in smoke. That was my chance. I applied for citizenship, said I was born in the United States, in San Francisco. What could they say? They had to believe me. Now it's *your* chance. I'm an American citizen now. I can bring my family back from China. I have no real son. You have no real father in America. So you will be my "paper son." Okay?

SAMMY LO (*nodding*)**:** Okay. Lin Shee lives in the third house, first row. She is a widow, no children, bound feet.

Scene 2: 1915, five months later, on Angel Island. Chin Li Chu is watching her friend Lois Wong knit.

CHIN LI CHU: How many sweaters have you made since you've been here?

LOIS WONG: Five. This makes six.

CHIN LI CHU: Will you teach me to knit? I'm going crazy, just sitting here waiting.

LOIS WONG: Don't be silly. Neither of us is going to be here long enough for me to teach you to knit.

CHIN LI CHU: How long have you been here?

LOIS WONG: Eight weeks.

CHIN LI CHU: I've been here six weeks. I don't think either of us is going anywhere soon, do you?

LOIS WONG: You must be optimistic. I'll tell you what. If you write a poem for me, I'll teach you how to knit.

(*They hear shouting from the men's section downstairs. Both women rush over to the windows to look out.*)

CHIN LI CHU: Look! They've released some of the men! Do you recognize anyone?

SAMMY LO (*calling from offstage*)**:** So long, Angel Island! So long, luk yi!

LOIS WONG: I recognize that voice—it's Yik Sem from my village. He was a farmer there. I wonder what he'll be here.

CHIN LI CHU: Why do you think they finally let him go? What's the right thing to say to make the luk yi let you go?

LOIS WONG: Aii, I wish I knew. Here, come sit by me, and I'll show you how to cast on. Wrap the yarn around your fingers like this—

(*The door opens, and Inspector Barnett enters the room. He looks around.*)

INSPECTOR BARNETT: Wei Shee! Wei Shee! (*He rubs his eyes as if he is crying.*)

WEI SHEE: No! No! You cannot send me back! My husband is here! I belong here with him! (*She tries to back away from Inspector Barnett, but he takes her by the arm.*)

INSPECTOR BARNETT: Chin Li Chu! Chin Li Chu!

CHIN LI CHU (*burying her face in her hands*)**:** Oh, no!

INSPECTOR BARNETT: Chin Li! Chin Li! *Sai gaai!* It's your lucky day!

LOIS WONG (*hugging Chin Li*)**:** Sai gaai! Good luck! You're free!

INSPECTOR BARNETT: Lois Wong! Lois Wong! Sai gaai to you, too!

EPILOGUE

Scene: Present day, Angel Island Immigration Station. Roy Ng and the Chu family are walking in the hall leading to what was once the basketball court at Angel Island. The walls are lined with handwritten poems in Chinese.

ROY NG: The wood is softer here than in the other rooms. It was easier to carve the poems here. But some people wrote in ink—one man even wrote poetry on the underside of his canvas cot! Soon it was hard to find space on the walls; the poems were everywhere, people expressing themselves on any surface they could find.

MAXINE CHU: It must have been so hard, waiting here. As beautiful and as sad as the poems are, I still can't imagine what it must have been like. Waiting here, not knowing if you would see your family again—in China or in the United States.

PAUL CHU: Paper sons waiting for paper permission to enter the country. Sammy Lo remained Sammy Lo. He was afraid to take back his name once he was admitted into the United States.

TINA CHU: Look! I've found it! I've found Chin Li's poem! "The west wind carries my thoughts to you." That's it, isn't it? That's the first line!

(*Everyone hurries over to Tina. They touch the wall carefully.*)

PAUL CHU: That's it. (*softly*) Chin Li was here.